NAKBA

Palestinians' Ongoing Dispossession

Sandra Watfa

NAKBA – Palestinians' Ongoing Dispossession

Author: Sandra Watfa

Copyright © Sandra Watfa (2023)

The right of Sandra Watfa to be identified as author of this work has been asserted by the author in accordance with section 77 and 78 of the Copyright, Designs and Patents Act 1988.

First Published in 2023

ISBN: 978-1-915996-13-8 (Hardback)

Book layout by:

White Magic Studios
www.whitemagicstudios.co.uk

Published by:

Maple Publishers
Fairbourne Drive, Atterbury,
Milton Keynes,
MK10 9RG, UK
www.maplepublishers.com

A CIP catalogue record for this title is available from the British Library.

All rights reserved. No part of this book may be reproduced or translated by any form or by any means, electronic or mechanical, including photocopying, recording or by any information storage and retrieval system without written permission from the author.

Bear in mind, it didn't start by accident; it started with plotting and planning and with Arthur Balfour giving away what was never his to give, started with lies, myths and an avalanche of dehumanisation and hate speech. When people stopped caring and became desensitised, they turned into collaborators.

A European-installed settler colony that resulted in the ethnic cleansing of over 750,000 Palestinians, the demolition of over 500 towns and villages, a plethora of massacres and a tsunami of ongoing war crimes and crimes against Humanity.

المرحوم جدعوده خليل وطفه
شهيد فلسطين

This book is dedicated to my great uncle
Jad'on Khalil Watfa
Assassinated by Zionist terrorists whilst defending Acre, Palestine
May 18th 1948

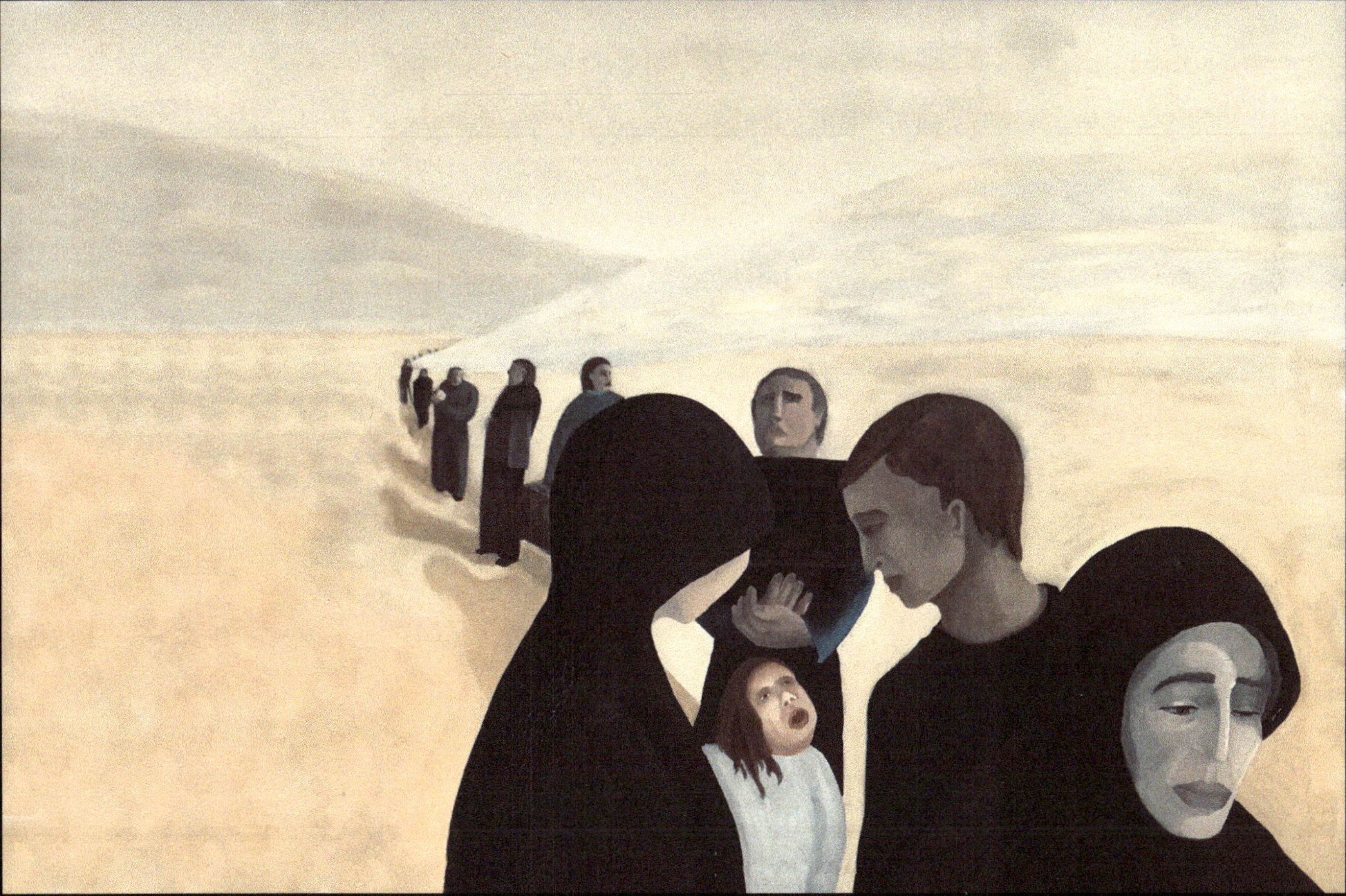

Solitary Confinement
Charcoal
2021

Keffiyeh
Charcoal

Guernigaza
Ink on paper
2018

Unbridled Loss
Charcoal
2021

Martyr
Charcoal
2022

NAKBA – Palestinians' Ongoing Dispossession

The Great March Of Return
Charcoal
2018

Zionist Architecture
Charcoal
2022

NAKBA – Palestinians' Ongoing Dispossession

Untitled
Charcoal
1997

Sandra Watfa

The Great March Of Return
Charcoal
2018

A Mother's Love
Pencil on paper
1995

Apartheid Wall
Pencil
2019

Naksa
Oil on canvas
1987

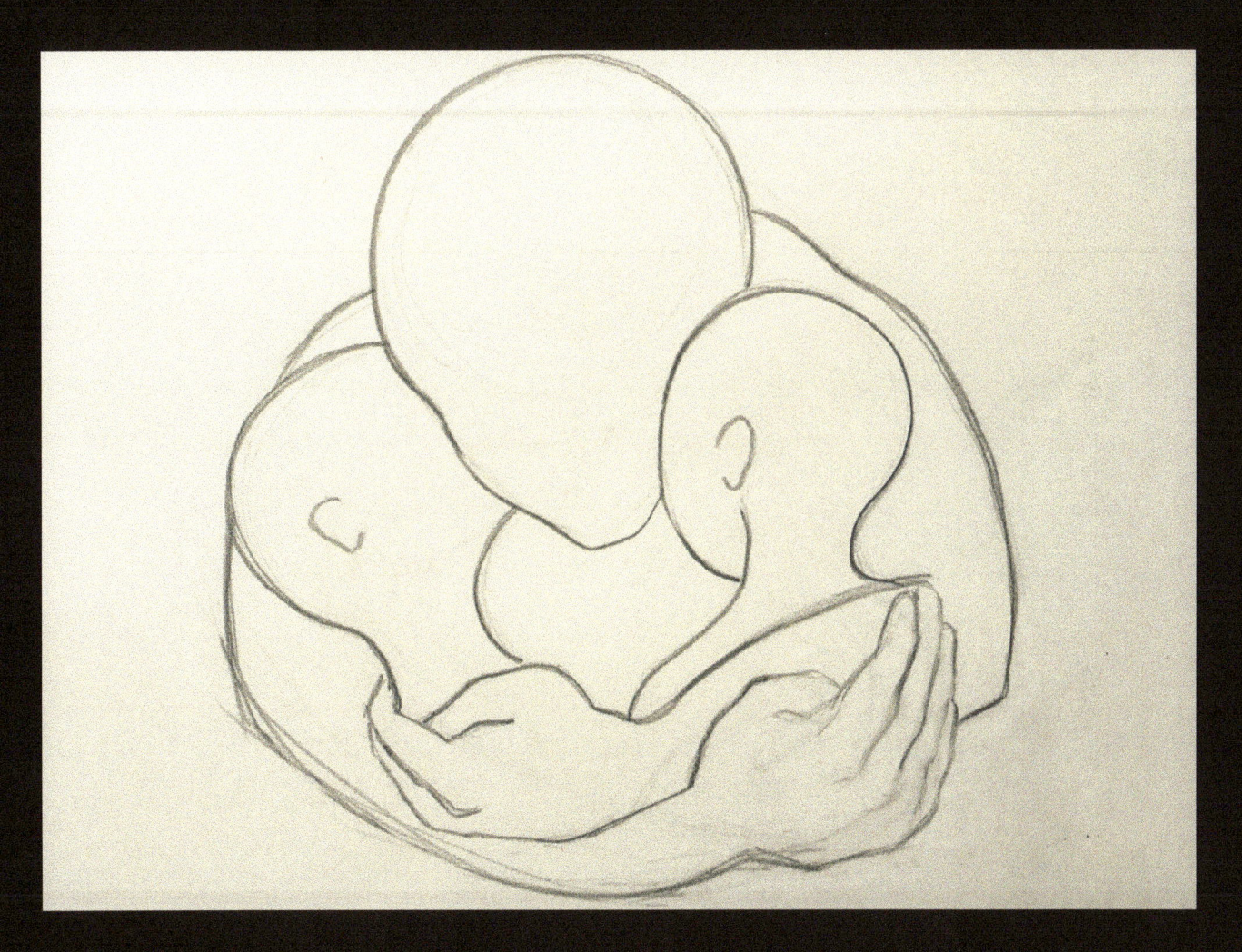

Protection
Pencil on paper
1997

Resilience
Charcoal and Pastel on paper
1991

Untitled
Charcoal
1999

Refugeedom
Charcoal
2021

Untitled
Graphite on paper
1998

Easter in the land of Christianity
Ink on paper

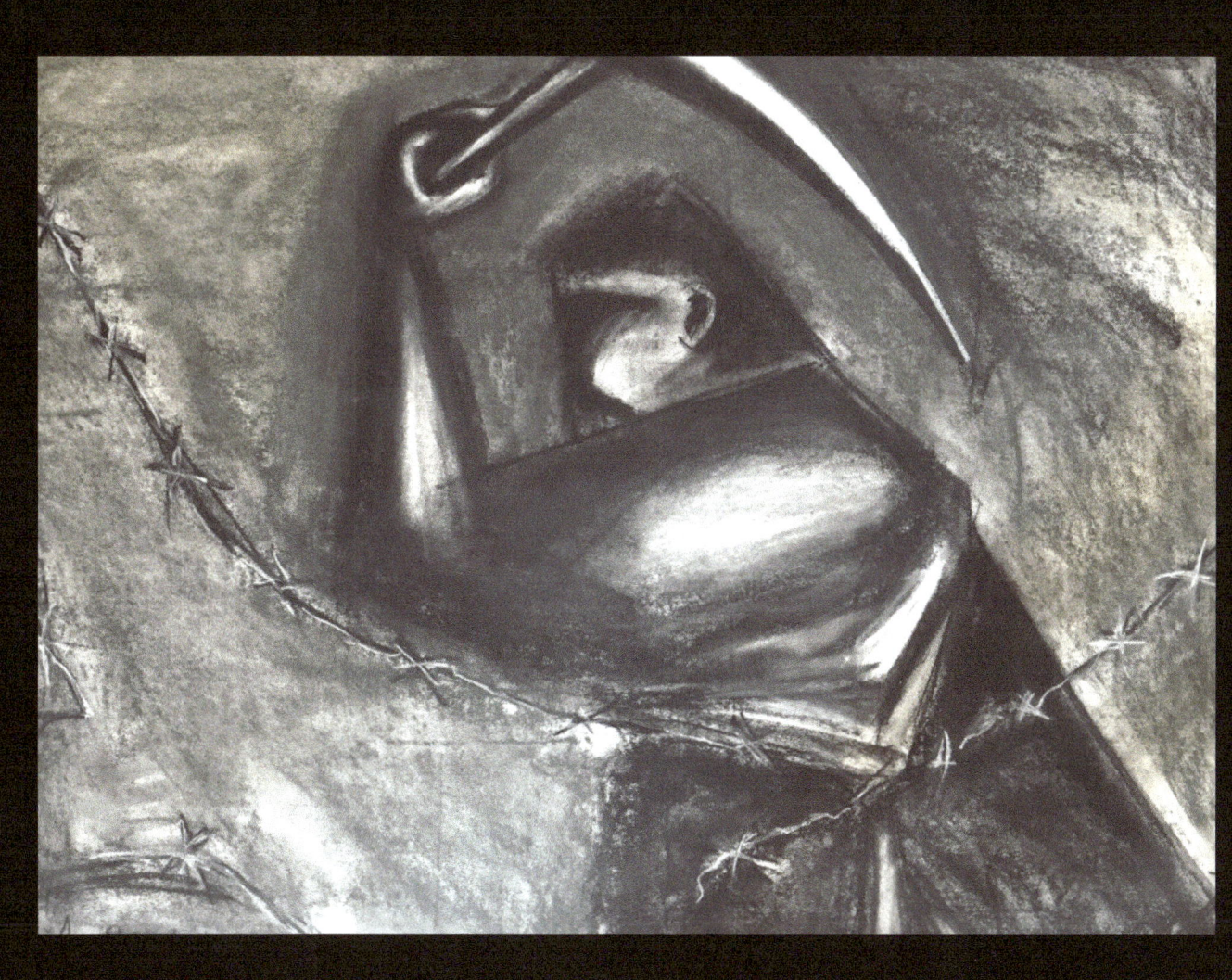

Breaking Out
Charcoal and graphite
1987

Life under siege
Charcoal
1989

Sandra Watfa

Administrative Detention
Charcoal
2005

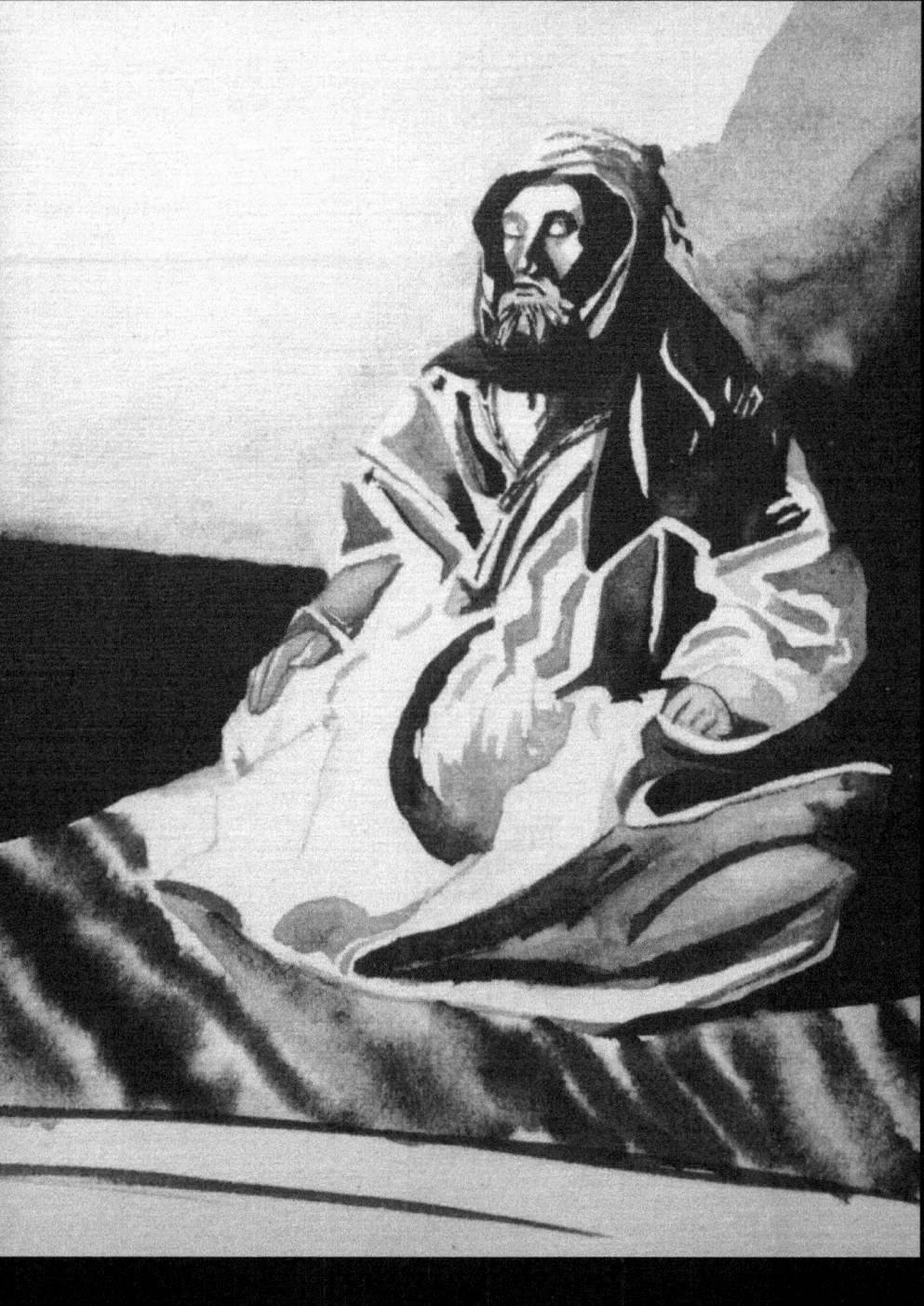

Zionist-Free Serenity
Ink on paper
1989

A State Born of Terror
Ink on paper
1987

Untitled
Charcoal
1988

Sandra Watfa

Nakba II
Charcoal
1994

Breaking Out II
Graphite on paper
1989

Untitled
Charcoal
1995

A Child's Death
Charcoal
1991

Christ Was A Palestinian
Charcoal
1996

The Futility Of War
Ink on paper
1989

Sketch
Ink on paper
2021

Mercy
Charcoal
1986

Sandra Watfa

Untitled
Charcoal
2006

Gaza, Open Air Poison
Etching
1988

A Mother's Pain
Charcoal
1988

Refugees II
Graphite on paper
1990

Skecth
Pencil
1993

Nakba, Sketch
Oil on paper
1985

Self Portrait
Oil on board
1985

Self Portrait
Charcoal
1986

Sandra Watfa

Childhood Stolen
Charcoal and Graphite on paper
1988

Refugees
Ink on paper
1990

Palestinian Child

He waits till three to go to sleep,
With heavy lids and aching limb.
He waits and thinks and starts to weep,
Recalling all that's been.

His father badly beaten, his mother on the floor,
Keening and beseeching them to
Let her young son go.

He waits till three and waits some more,
Awaits the shock of the knock on the door;
Heralding a scene of a mad war crime,
A crime, in truth, which all ignore.

Snatched and flung in hell and beyond,
His innocence shafted, his childhood gone.
He waits till three to go to sleep,

And while he waits, his freedom's gone.

Palestinian Child
Charcoal
2017

Check the Intent

I have seen
the invisible
heard the inaudible
eaten the inedible and
lived the unliveable.
Been plucked and
thrust and
flung from
pillar
to post,
cussed and
dissed and
shunned
by most
Though my feet stand
on foreign soil,
my sight is fixed on
alighting Home;
To all who have
traded in
my country's name,
and tried to fix
themselves in vain
checking the label, not
the Intent:
pick someone else's cause
and vent.
sixty eight years are
quite enough
to go it
alone,
accompanied by no one's shadow
but one's own.

Sandra Watfa

Check the Intent
Charcoal
2017

Suggested reading list

- Palestine Is Our Home, Voices of Loss, Courage and Steadfastness, Nahida Halaby Gordon, editor
- Mornings In Jenin, Susan Abulhawa
- On Zionist Colonisation, Ghassan Kanafani
- Rifqa, Mohammed El Kurd
- The Ethnic Cleansing Of Palestine, Ilan Pappe
- A State Of Terror, Thomas Suarez
- Before Their Diaspora, Walid Khalidi
- Eyes In Gaza, Mads Gilbert and Erik Fosse
- Out Of Place, Edward Said
- Palestine the Reality, The Inside Story Of The Balfour Declaration 1917-1938, JMN Jeffries
- In Search Of Fatima, Ghada Karmi
- The Hundred Years War On Palestine, Rashid Khalidi
- A Four Thousand Year History, Nur Masalha
- Justice For Some, Noura Erakat
- A River Dies Of Thirst, Mahmoud Darwish
- Returning To Haifa, Ghassan Kanafani
- Against Our Better Judgement, Alison Weir